In the name of Allah, the Entirely Merciful,
the Especially Merciful.

Copyright © 2019 Ad-Duha Institute, Inc.
4th Edition
Baltimore, Maryland, USA
www.ad-duha.org
support@ad-duha.org

All Rights Reserved

No part of this publication may be reproduced, stored in any retrieval system, or transmitted in any form or by any means, electronic, mechanical, photocopying, recording or otherwise, without the prior written permission of Ad-Duha Institute, Inc. Any right not specifically mentioned herein is reserved by Ad-Duha Institute.

Ad-Duha's mission is to help Muslim families provide their children with quality Islamic materials. Therefore, we ask that our customers help us in this task by honoring the copyright (i.e., not making copies or posting online) of our products.

This copyright is intended to ensure that the school can stay financially viable (i.e., cover the costs of development, production, and marketing) through the legitimate sale of its products. Honoring the rights of everyone, including those of your Muslim brothers/sisters, is sacred in Islaam.

If you would like to learn more about copyright law in Islaam, please visit our web site (click on "Terms of Use" at the bottom of any page) for a comprehensive summary of the Fatwa (religious ruling issued by scholars) regarding this matter.

ISBN-13: 978-1-64561-084-7

Printed in the United States of America

How to Use These Books

The Mini Tafseer Book Series is designed to teach children the Tafseer (exegesis) of all the suwaar (chapters) in the 30th Part of the Qur'aan. Each book in this 38-book series covers a different surah. The books feature:

- Special facts about the surah
- Arabic text of the surah
- English transliteration (to assist non-Arabic speakers)
- English translation
- Simplified Tafseer
- Illustrations/Coloring pages (no animals/humans)
- Highlighted Arabic vocabulary
- Sahih Ahadith
- One sentence summary of what the surah is about
- Review section
- Notes on the text (additional facts and information)

Teaching Tips:

If your younger child has trouble going through the whole book in one sitting, or does not retain all of the information taught, then just focus on the Tafseer pages first (i.e., those that explain the verses of the surah) and save the additional information contained in the Quick Facts, What's Special, Asbaab An-Noozool, and Vocabulary sections* for later when your child has mastered the Tafseer.

For older or advanced students who need more of a challenge, you can take time to go through all sections and discuss the lesson notes for that section (located at the end of the text). This will make lessons more challenging and provide a deeper understanding of the Tafseer, and Allah knows best.

*Some books may not contain all of these sections.

Mini Tafseer Book Series
Suratun-Naba'

Quick Facts about Suratun-Naba

Suratun-Naba' was revealed in **Makkah**. Thus, Suratun-Naba' (like all other suwaar revealed in Makkah) is called a **'Makki'** surah.

Suratun-Naba' gets its name from the word **An-Naba'**, meaning 'The News' which is used in the second ayah.

Suratun-Naba' is also known by the name **'Am-ma**, because that is the first word in the surah.

What is Suratun-Naba' all about?

Suratun-Naba' tells us that disbelievers **argue about Yowmul-Qiyaamah**, but Allah shows them in the creation that He is **capable of doing everything He intends**.

Now let's learn what makes Suratun-Naba' so...

Suratun-Naba' is so special because?

It is the **first surah** in the **30th Juz'** of the Qur'an!

You see, many people like to read the whole Qur'aan in **one month**, especially in the month of **Ramadaan**.

Therefore, the Qur'aan was divided into **30 equal parts**, so that reading the entire Qur'aan in one month would be easy; **one part each day**.

In Arabic, each of these parts is called a **Jooz'**, two parts are called **Jooz'ayn**, and three or more parts are called **Ajzaa'**.

All thirty Ajzaa' in the Qur'aan have a number (from 1-30), as well as a name based on the **first ayah of the first surah** in that particular Jooz'.

That is why the 30th Jooz' is also more commonly known as, **Jooz' 'Amma** after the first word in Suratun-Naba', which is the first surah in that Jooz'. That makes Suratun-Naba' very special indeed.

So now you know!

Now let's get ready to learn what Suratun-Naba' is all about!

We will start by learning **9 new words** from the Qur'aan.

The more words you know from the Qur'aan, the better you will understand each surah that you learn insha-Allah.

Understanding the Qur'aan is what Allah wants us to do!

So, let's get started right now!

9 NEW WORDS!

Vocabulary List

Keep a look out for the following vocabulary words while you read! These words will help you remember the meaning of Suratun-Naba', insha-Allah!

the news
(i.e., The Day of Judgment)

ٱلنَّبَإِ

(an-na-ba')

wide expanse

مِهَٰدًا

(me-haa-daa)

pegs

أَوْتَادًا

(ow-taa-daa)

pairs

أَزْوَٰجًا

(az-waa-jaa)

rest	سُبَاتًا	(soo-baa-taa)
livelihood	مَعَاشًا	(ma-'aa-shaa)
seven	سَبْعًا	(sub-un)
ambush	مِرْصَادًا	(mir-saw-daa)
destination	مَءَابًا	(ma-'aa-baa)

Now that we are ready,
we need to start the right way...

There are **two things** we should say before we start reading a surah from the Qur'aan. Can you remember what they are?

#1 We say the Isti'aathah[1]...

I seek refuge with Allah from the cursed Shaytaan.

('A-'oo-thoo-bil-laa-he-me-nash-shay-taa-nir-ra-jeem)

أَعُوذُ بِاللهِ مِنَ الشَّيْطَانِ الرَّجِيمِ

We start reading Qur'aan by asking Allah to protect us from Shaytaan and...

#2 We say the Basmallah[2]...

In the name of Allah, the Beneficent, the Merciful.

(Bis-mil-laa-hir-rah-maa-nir-ra-heem)

We remember Allah and say how great He is for giving us so many wonderful blessings!

We are ready to go now! You know your **new words** and you've said the **Isti'aathah** and **Basmallah**...

Now it is time to learn what
Suratun-Naba' says...

"About what are they asking one another?"
('am-ma ya-ta-saa-a-loon)

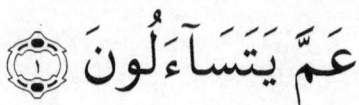

"About the great news,"
('a-nin-na-ba-il-'a-theem)

"That over which they are in disagreement."
(Al-la-thee hoom fee-hee mookh-ta-lee-foon)

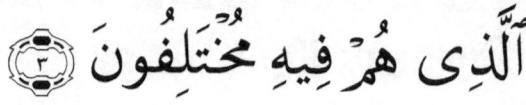

"No! They are going to know."
(Kal-laa sa-ya'-la-moon)

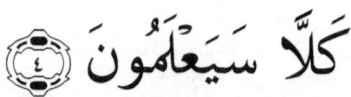

"Then, no! They are going to know."
(Thoom-ma kal-laa sa-ya'-la-moon)

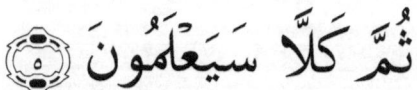

When Rasulullahﷺ told his people, the Quraysh, about Yowmul-Qiyaamah (The Day of Judgment), they started **arguing about whether it would really happen or not.**

People do the same thing nowadays when they are told that Yowmul-Qiyaamah is coming.

They get so busy arguing about something that they have no knowledge of, they fail to see that all their arguments are just **conjecture and wishful thinking.**

It would be better to spend that time **preparing for the day instead.**

So, Allah asks the disbelievers the following **rhetorical question** (that means a question Allah already knows the answer to), so that they will **stop arguing and start preparing.** He asks them...

"What are you arguing about, is it the Great News?"

Allah calls Yowmul-Qiyaamah 'An-Naba'il-Adheem,' meaning 'The Great News,' **because** this day will be the most important event in all of creation, it is the **most important news that anyone will ever hear about.**

Allah wants them to realize that arguing about something that they have no knowledge of is **useless**.

What's really important is that this day is coming, and Allah tells the deniers in these ayaat that they will surely be **convinced when they see it**, but then it will be **too late.**

In the coming ayaat, Allah will teach us **11 examples** from His creation that prove He is indeed **more than capable** of making Yowmul-Qiyaamah happen.

"Have We not made the earth a resting place,"

(A-lam naj-'a-lil-ar-da mee-haa-daa)

1

Allah created the **earth** secure and comfortable for us, like a bed.

So, isn't Allah capable of making something as great as Yowmul-Qiyaamah, too?

"And the mountains as stakes,"

(Wal-jee-baa-loo ow-taa-daa)

وَٱلْجِبَالَ أَوْتَادًا ٧

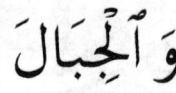

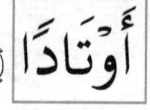

Allah has made the **mountains** like stakes to stabilize the earth, so we can walk and build upon it safely.

So, isn't Allah capable of making something as great as Yowmul-Qiyaamah, too?

"And We created you in pairs,"

(Wa-kha-laq-naa-koom az-waa-jaa)

 وَخَلَقْنَٰكُمْ أَزْوَٰجًا

Allah has **made us in pairs**, male and female, so that we can get married and have children.

So, isn't Allah capable of making something as great as Yowmul-Qiyaamah, too?

"And made your sleep (as a means for) rest,"

(Wa-ja-'al-naa now-ma-koom soo-baa-taa)

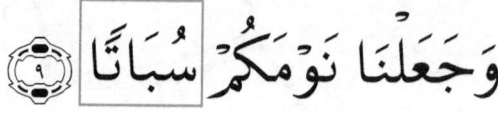

Allah has given us **sleep**, so that we can rest and our bodies can repair themselves.

So, isn't Allah capable of making something as great as Yowmul-Qiyaamah, too?

"And made the night as a clothing (covering),"

(Wa-ja-'al-nal-lay-la lee-baa-saa)

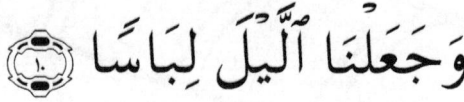

Allah has made the **night**, covering us in darkness, as a tranquil time to take a break from the activities of the day.

So, isn't Allah capable of making something as great as Yowmul-Qiyaamah, too?

"And made the day for livelihood?"

(Wa-ja-'al-nan-na-haa-ra ma-'aa-shaa)

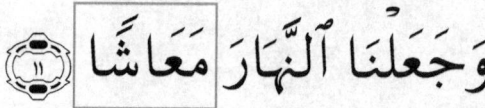

Allah has made the **day** for us to be active and get our work done.

So, isn't Allah capable of making something as great as Yowmul-Qiyaamah, too?

"And constructed above you seven strong (heavens),"

(Wa-ba-nay-naa fow-qa-koom sab-'an shee-daa-daa)

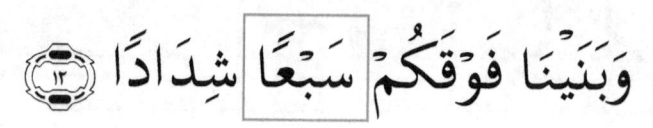

وَبَنَيْنَا فَوْقَكُمْ سَبْعًا شِدَادًا ۝

Allah has made the **sky**, which has seven strong levels above us.

So, isn't Allah capable of making something as great as Yowmul-Qiyaamah, too?

"And made (therein) a burning lamp,"

(Wa-ja-'al-naa see-raa-jow-wah-haa-jaa)

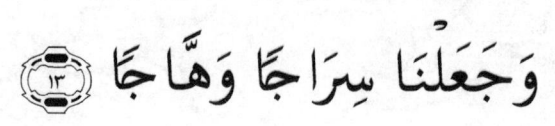

وَجَعَلْنَا سِرَاجًا وَهَّاجًا ﴿١٣﴾

Allah has made the **sun** to give us both light and warmth. The sun's light makes it possible for us to see clearly during the day, keeps the earth just the right temperature, and makes plants grow.

So, isn't Allah capable of making something as great as Yowmul-Qiyaamah, too?

"And sent down from the rain clouds, pouring water,"
(Wa-an-zal-naa mee-nal-moo'-see-raa-tee maa-un thaj-jaa-jaa)

وَأَنزَلْنَا مِنَ ٱلْمُعْصِرَٰتِ مَآءً ثَجَّاجًا ۝

Allah has made the **rain** flowing from the clouds. The rain gives us water to drink and wash with, as well as water for our crops and animals.

So, isn't Allah capable of making something as great as Yowmul-Qiyaamah, too?

"That We may bring forth thereby grain and vegetation,"

(Lee-nookh-ree-ja bee-hee hab-bow-wa-na-baa-taa)

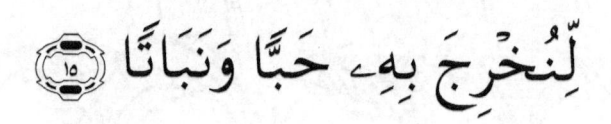

لِنُخْرِجَ بِهِۦ حَبًّا وَنَبَاتًا ﴿١٥﴾

10

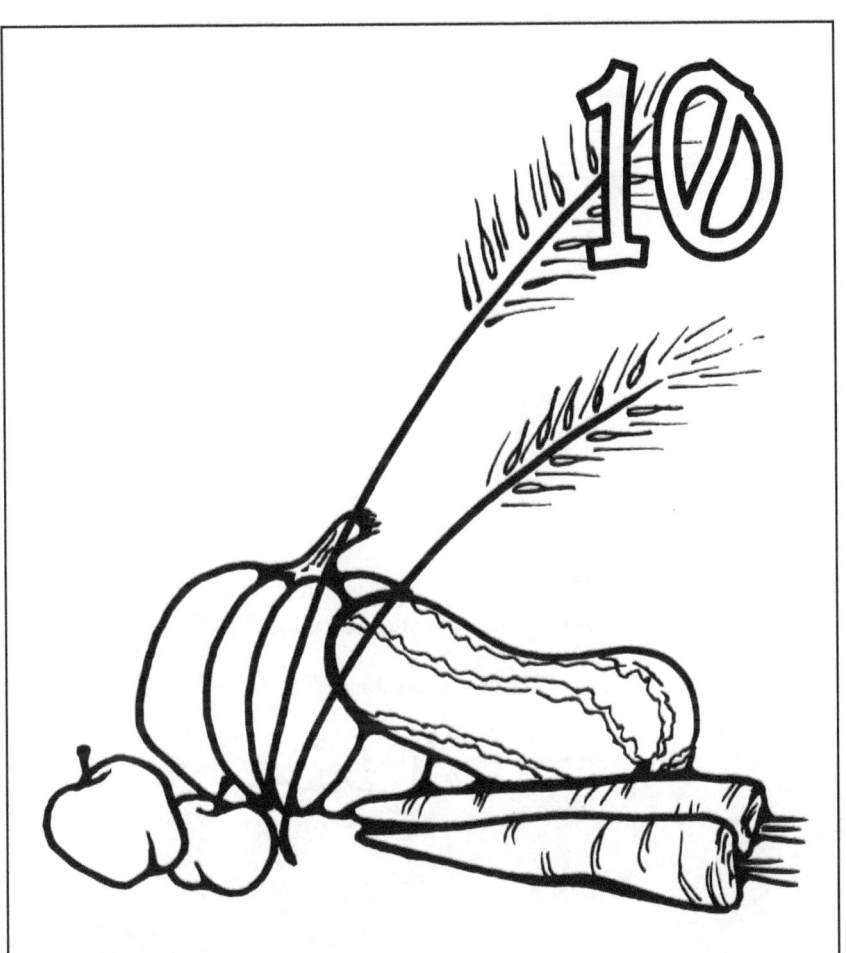

Allah has given us **grain and vegetables**, an enormous variety of healthy, delicious foods to enjoy and benefit from.
This includes those that we dry, and keep for latter use, as well as those that are eaten fresh.

So, isn't Allah capable of making something as great as Yowmul-Qiyaamah, too?

"And gardens of entwined growth?"

(Wa-jan-naa-tin al-faa-faa)

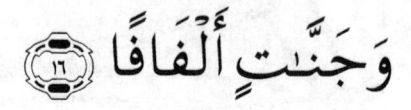

وَجَنَّٰتٍ أَلْفَافًا ﴿١٦﴾

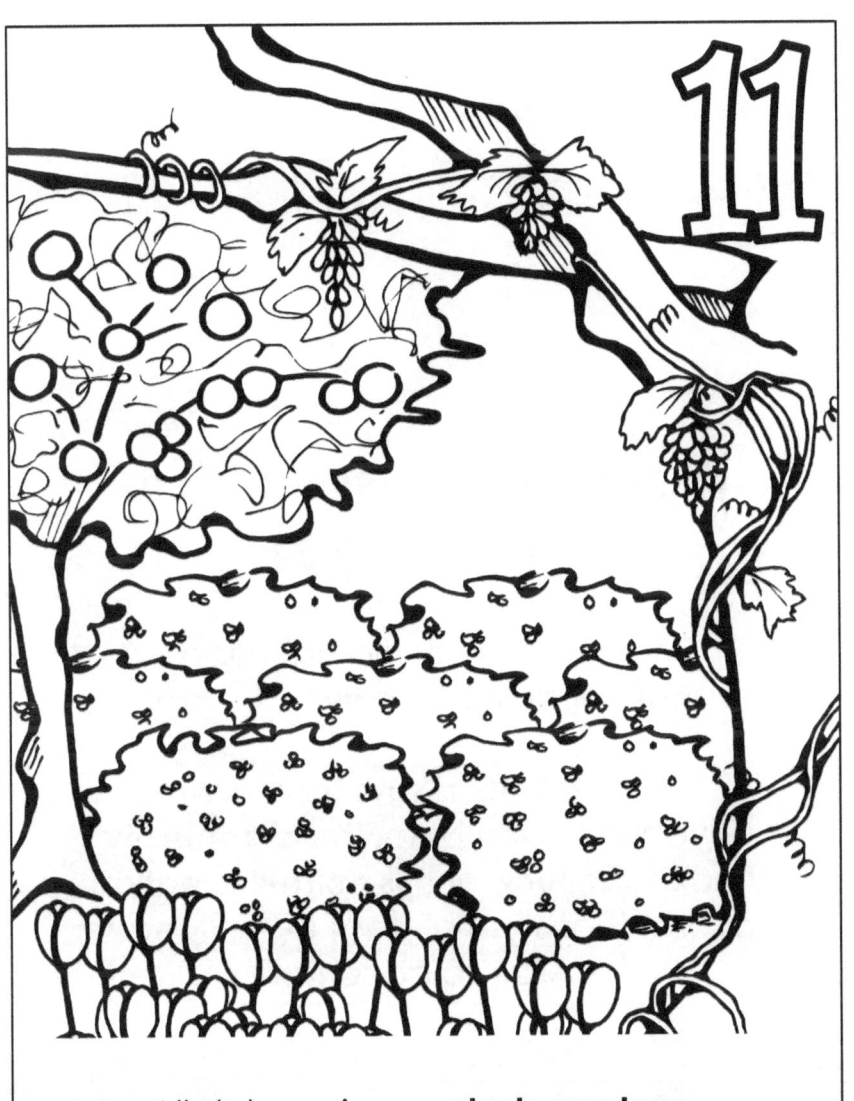

Allah has given us **lush gardens**, growing thick with all manner of fruits, flowers, and herbs to benefit us.

So, isn't Allah capable of making something as great as Yowmul-Qiyaamah, too?

Why does Allah mention all of these examples?

Because they show that Allah is **capable of doing whatever He intends.**

Therefore, if Allah says that Yowmul-Qiyaamah will come, the **complexity and magnitude of this current creation** proves that such a great event is easy for Allah to accomplish.

Now that the examples are done, it is time to learn what will happen on Yowmul-Qiyaamah, **so we know what is really in store...**

"Indeed, the Day of Judgment is an appointed time,"

(In-na yow-mal-fas-lee kaa-na mee-qaa-taa)

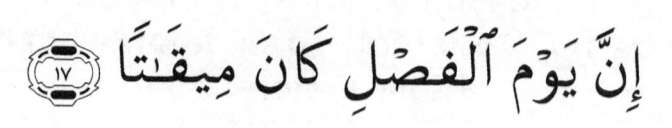

إِنَّ يَوْمَ ٱلْفَصْلِ كَانَ مِيقَٰتًا ﴿١٧﴾

Yowmul-Qiyaamah is already scheduled to happen at a certain time, **not a second sooner or later**.

This decree has been set by Allah, and **only Allah knows the exact time**.

Neither the disbelievers, nor any other creation has knowledge of the time, and no one will ever find out. We will only know for sure the moment it actually happens.

"The Day that the horn is blown, and you will come forth in multitudes (i.e., crowds);"

(Yow-ma yoon-fa-khoo fees-soo-ree fa-ta'-too-na af-wa-jaa)

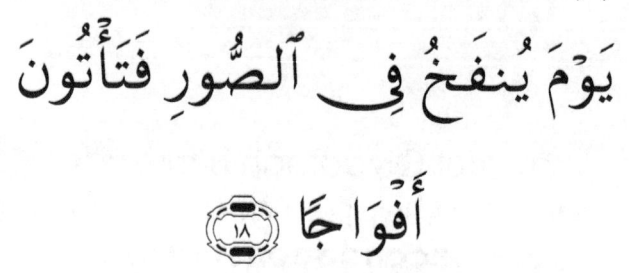

يَوْمَ يُنفَخُ فِى ٱلصُّورِ فَتَأْتُونَ أَفْوَاجًا ﴿١٨﴾

"And the heaven is opened and will become gateways,"

(Wa-foo-tee-ha-tis-sa-maa-oo fa-kaa-nut ab-waa-baa)

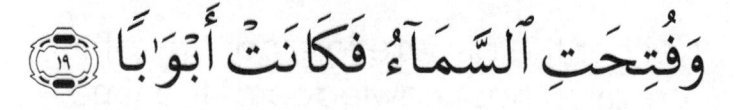

وَفُتِحَتِ ٱلسَّمَآءُ فَكَانَتْ أَبْوَٰبًا ﴿١٩﴾

"And the mountains are removed and will be (but) a mirage."

(Wa-sooy-yee-ra-til-jee-baa-loo fa-kaa-nut sa-raa-baa)

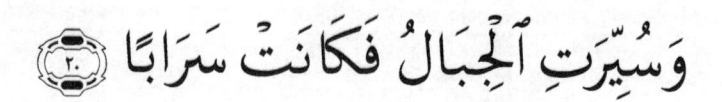

وَسُيِّرَتِ ٱلْجِبَالُ فَكَانَتْ سَرَابًا ﴿٢٠﴾

Yowmul-Qiyaamah will start with the **blowing of the horn** by Angel Israfeel.

When it is blown everyone will be **resurrected**, then the **heavens will open** up, and the **mountains will disappear**.

The earth will be a flat, wide plain, and we will all be gathered there for judgment.

"Indeed, Hell has been lying in wait,"

(Inna jahannama kanat mirsadan)

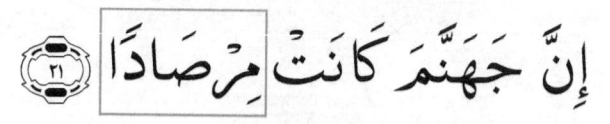

إِنَّ جَهَنَّمَ كَانَتْ مِرْصَادًا ﴿٢١﴾

"For the transgressors a place of return:"

(Lilttagheena maaban)

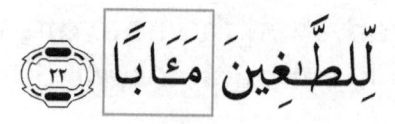

لِّلطَّاغِينَ مَآبًا ﴿٢٢﴾

"In which they will remain for ages (unending)."

(Laa-bee-theena fee-ha ah-qaa-baa)

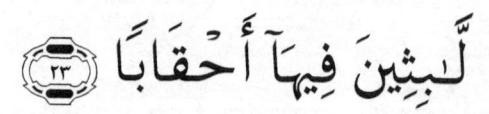

لَّابِثِينَ فِيهَآ أَحْقَابًا ﴿٢٣﴾

Jahannam has been prepared for the disbelievers, and they will see it clearly on that day. Once they enter there, they will stay **forever**.

Some people say it's okay if they go to Jahannam because they will only be there for **a few days**.

Even if what they say was true (and it's not), time in Jahannam is not the same as time the way we know it. Each day in Jahannam is **much longer** than our whole life, and each year is much longer than we could even count!

That is not all, there is **more punishment** Allah will inform us of in the next ayaat...

"They will not taste therein (any) coolness or drink,"

(Laa ya-thoo-qoo-na fee-haa bar-dan wa-laa sha-raa-baa)

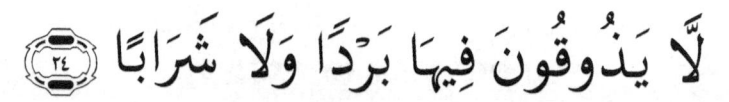

لَّا يَذُوقُونَ فِيهَا بَرْدًا وَلَا شَرَابًا ﴿٢٤﴾

"Except scalding water and (foul) purulence (a fluid, dark, murky, intensely cold),"

(Il-laa ha-mee-mun wa-ghas-saa-qaa)

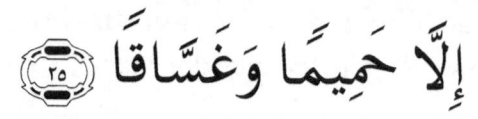

إِلَّا حَمِيمًا وَغَسَّاقًا ﴿٢٥﴾

The dwellers of Jahannam will have nothing to drink except **two fluids**...

BOILING WATER
&
intensely cold, putrid liquid

The boiling water will **burn their insides**, while the intensely cold, putrid liquid comes from the **sweat, tears, and pus from the infected wounds** of the people of Jahannam.

This drink smells bad, is dark in color, and will not quench their thirst at all.

This is what the people will drink in Jahannam, **may Allah save us from this punishment.**

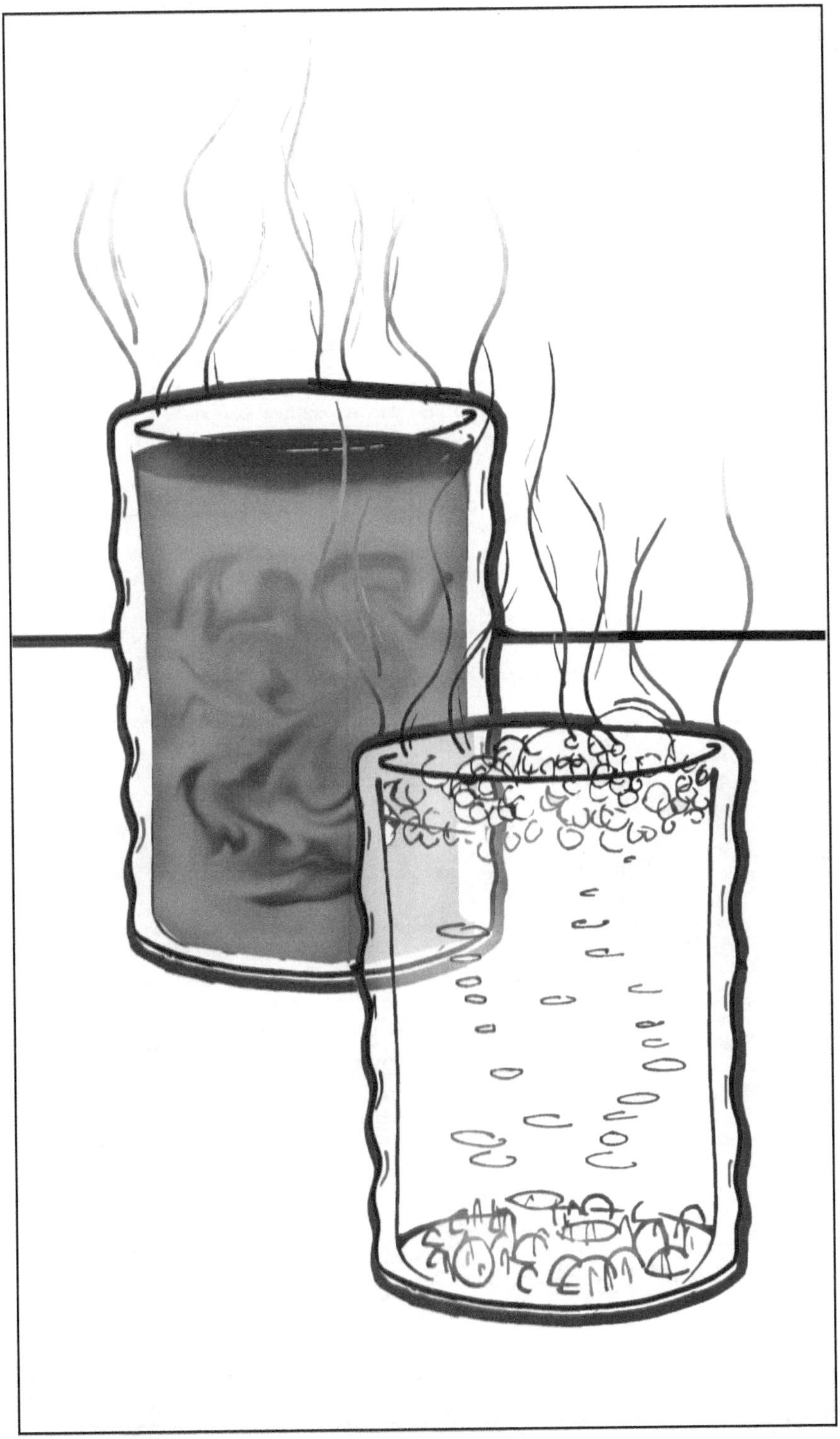

"An appropriate recompense."

(Ja-zaa-ow-wee-faa-qaa)

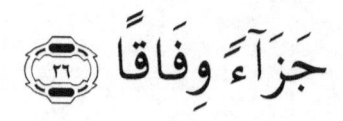

جَزَآءً وِفَاقًا ﴿٢٦﴾

"Indeed, they were not expecting an account (of their deeds),"

(In-na-hoom kaa-noo laa yar-joo-na hee-saa-baa)

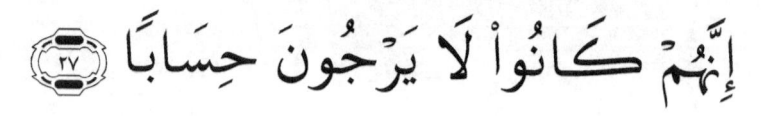

إِنَّهُمْ كَانُوا لَا يَرْجُونَ حِسَابًا ﴿٢٧﴾

"And denied our verses with (emphatic) denial."

(Wa-kath-tha-boo bee-aa-yaa-tee-naa kith-thaa-baa)

وَكَذَّبُوا بِآيَاتِنَا كِذَّابًا ﴿٢٨﴾

"But all things We have enumerated in writing."

(Wa-kool-la shay-in ah-say-naa-hoo kee-taa-baa)

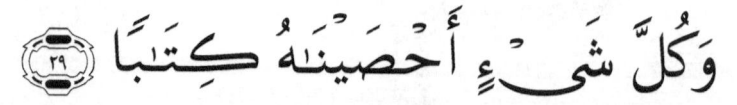

وَكُلَّ شَيْءٍ أَحْصَيْنَاهُ كِتَابًا ﴿٢٩﴾

"So, taste (the penalty), and never will We increase you except in torment."

(Fa-thoo-qoo fa-lan na-zee-da-koom il-laa 'a-thaa-baa)

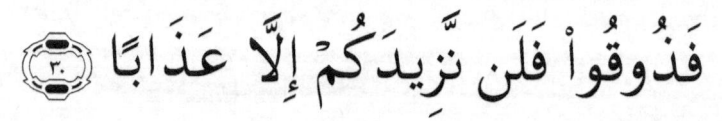

فَذُوقُوا فَلَن نَزِيدَكُمْ إِلَّا عَذَابًا ﴿٣٠﴾

Allah tells us this is the right punishment...

Those who go to Jahannam will be there because they **did not prepare** for Yowmul-Qiyaamah.

To be ready for Yowmul-Qiyaamah, a person needs to follow Allah's guidance, and live a **good life as defined by Allah**, not by our own personal beliefs and whims.

But those who will be in Jahannam **denied** Yowmul-Qiyaamah in this life and **argued** about Allah's message.

Everything that Allah plans, He has put in a **written record**, no exceptions. Yowmul-Qiyaamah is in this written record, and those who deny it, instead of getting the good they expect from Allah, will only get an increase in their punishment because they did not take Allah's laws seriously.

How is that fair?

You may be wondering why Allah would punish people so severely just because they did not worship Him and prepare for Yowmul-Qiyaamah.

After all, they may have **meant well**, or expected that Allah would **have mercy** on them for not realizing the truth.

Well, let's look at a story that will help you understand why this punishment is actually **fair and just**.

The Careless Farmer

Imagine there is a **farmer** who inherits a **large fertile farm**. He moves his family to the farm and thinks that life will now be happy and easy for him. What he does not realize is that having a farm is a lot of **hard work and planning.**

The other farmers in his town know that without a good harvest, their families will **starve** (because they have no food) and they will **lose their farms** (because they cannot pay the bills), so they take the job of farming **seriously.**

The farmers must work long hours, invest money for the proper supplies, and learn everything there is to know about farming in order to get the **best and biggest harvest.**

The problem is, **this particular farmer is careless**. He does not believe anything bad can happen to him or his farm.

Because of his strong belief that he does not have to work hard; the farmer makes **mistakes** throughout the growing season that will lead to **terrible consequences at harvest time.**

First, he plants the wrong seeds, and does not water them regularly. Then he fails to pull out the weeds, and allows insects to infest his crops.

Eventually, his fellow farmers, who all have fields full of ripening fruit and vegetables, **warn him** that his plants will never bear fruit. But he **argues** with them about things he has no knowledge of.

When **harvest time** comes in the fall, the farmer harvests his plants and takes them to market, but no one will buy his piles **of insect laden leaves and hardy weeds.**

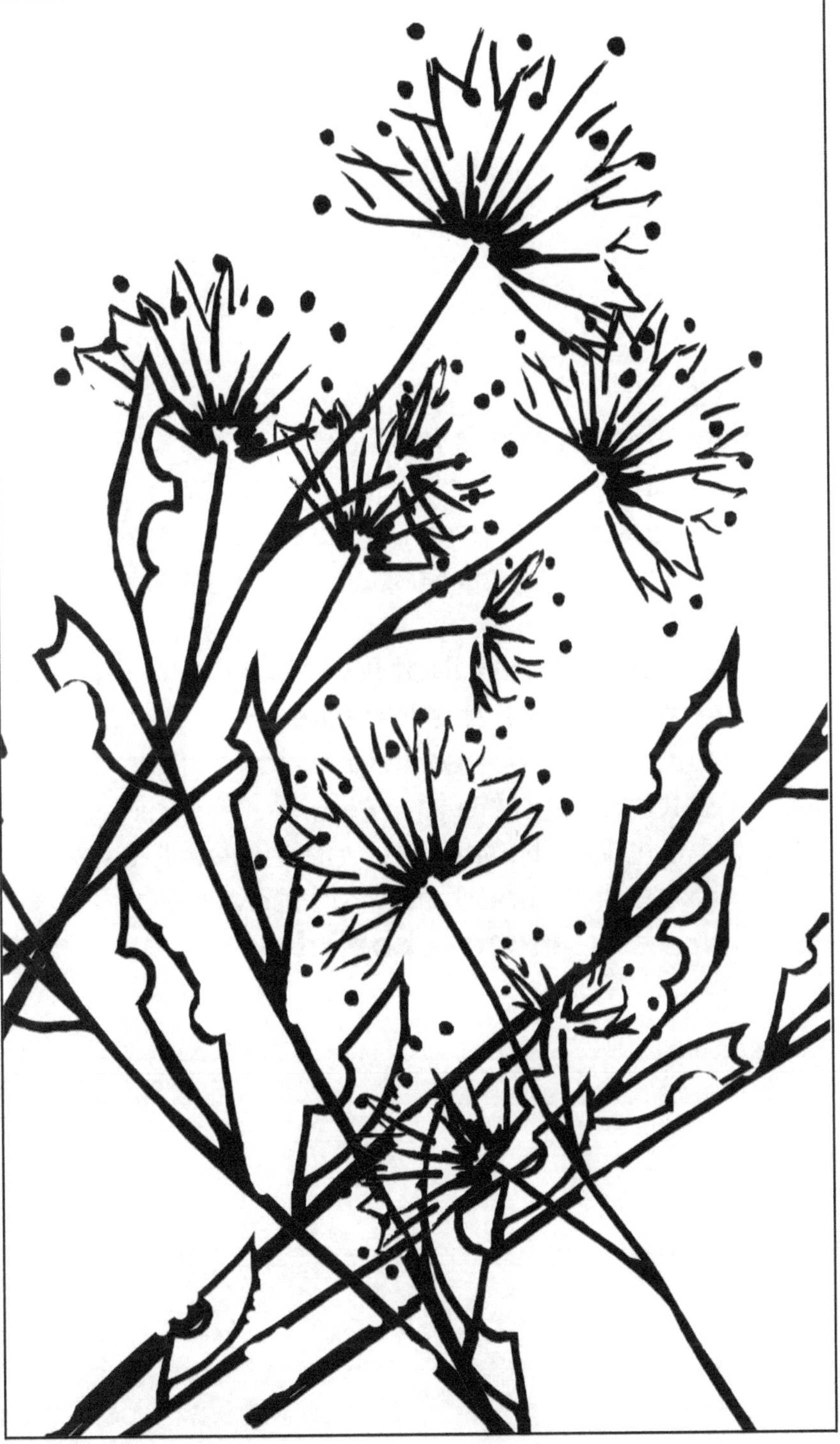

Now the farmer is **terrified** that his family will **starve** through the winter, and he will **lose his farm** because he has no money to buy food or pay bills.

He now realizes that **his fellow farmers were right, but it is too late.** He did not put in the work needed to take care of the farm, and he ignored the warnings of his fellow farmers, so now he will lose everything he has, just because of **incorrect beliefs.**

Is what happened to the farmer unfair or unjust?

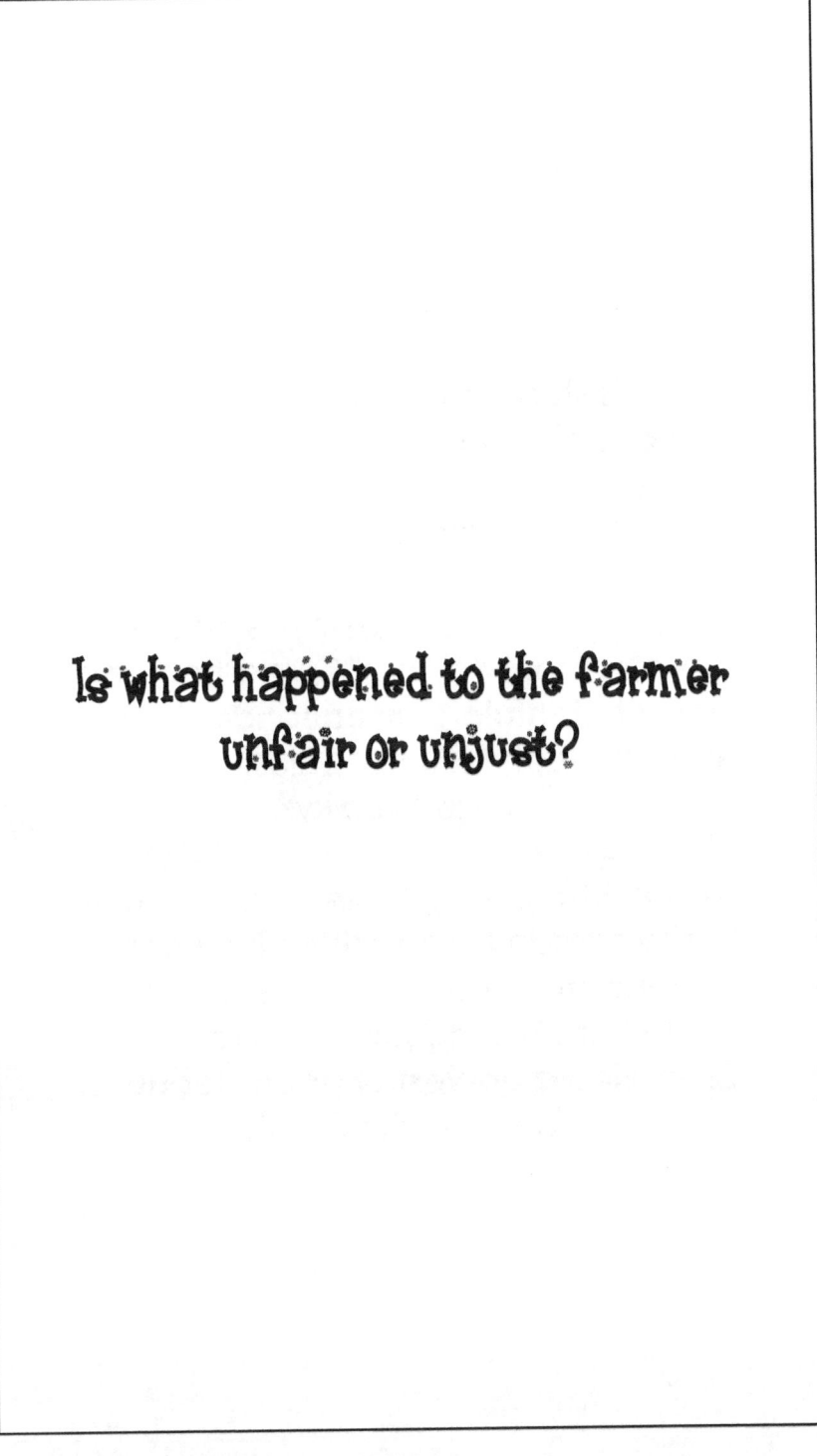

This story shows us that having **incorrect beliefs** can lead to terrible consequences in this life, and this is not unjust or unfair, it is just reality.

In the same way, a person's incorrect beliefs about Yowmul-Qiyaamah can lead to **terrible consequences in the next life**, but this is not unjust or unfair, it is just reality.

Those who do not believe in Yowmul-Qiyaamah think **nothing bad can happen to them** because of their beliefs. The disbelievers are not preparing a **harvest of good deeds** for Yowmul-Qiyaamah.

They are not doing **Salaah** (5 daily prayers), **Sowm** (fasting), and Zakaah (giving charity), nor are they staying away from the things that Allah has made **Haraam**, like alcohol and swine.

So, just like the farmer with the bad harvest had nothing good to sell at the market after the harvest, they will have **nothing good to put on their scale** to earn Jannah, or to protect them from Jahannam, on Yowmul-Qiyaamah.

"Indeed, for the Righteous is attainment (fulfillment of the heart's desires);"
(In-na lil-moot-ta-qee-na ma-faa-zaa)

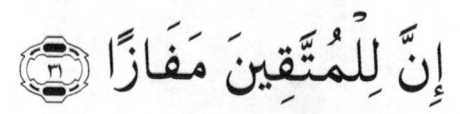

إِنَّ لِلْمُتَّقِينَ مَفَازًا ﴿٣١﴾

"Gardens and grapevines;"
(Ha-da-ee-qa wa-a'-naa-baa)

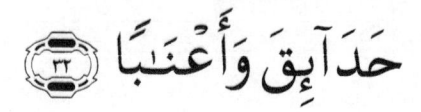

حَدَائِقَ وَأَعْنَابًا ﴿٣٢﴾

"And full-bosomed (companions) of equal age;"
(Wa-ka-waa-'ee-ba at-raa-baa)

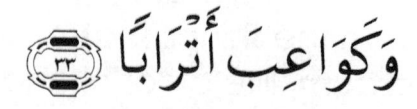

وَكَوَاعِبَ أَتْرَابًا ﴿٣٣﴾

"And a full cup."
(Wa-ka'-sun dee-haa-qaa)

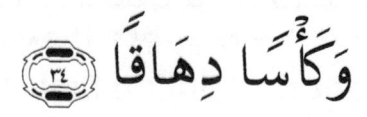

وَكَأْسًا دِهَاقًا ﴿٣٤﴾

"No ill speech will they hear therein, or falsehood:"
(Laa yas-ma-'oo-na fee-haa lagh-wow-wa-laa kith-tha-baa)

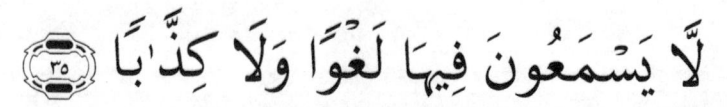

لَّا يَسْمَعُونَ فِيهَا لَغْوًا وَلَا كِذَّابًا ﴿٣٥﴾

"(As) reward from your Lord, (a generous) gift, (made due) by account,"
(Ja-zaa-am-mir-rab-bee-ka 'a-taa-an hee-saa-baa)

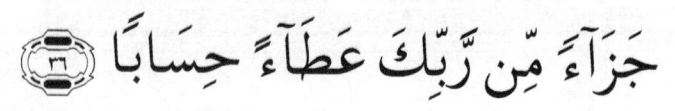

جَزَاءً مِّن رَّبِّكَ عَطَاءً حِسَابًا ﴿٣٦﴾

What about the believers?

The situation for those who have **correct beliefs** about Allah, and who do the **hard work** to get ready for Yowmul-Qiyaamah, will be very different.

Just like the **careful farmers**, who followed the rules and had good harvests, the believers who follow Allah's rules will come on Yowmul-Qiyaamah with **scales full of good deeds.**

They will enter Jannah and be given **everything that their hearts desire**. They will have lush gardens to live in, delicious fruits to eat, beautiful companions of the same age to live with, cups to drink from that never empty, and they will never hear anyone saying bad things or lying (like what they used to hear in this life).

The people who get this reward will be so happy, that they will never want anything else, and **they will enjoy this reward forever.**

"(From) the Lord of the heavens and the earth, and whatever is between them, the Most Merciful. They possess not from Him (authority for) speech."

(Rab-bis-sa-maa-waa-tee wal-ar-dee wa-maa bay-na-hoo-mar-rah-maa-nee laa yum-lee-koo-na min-hoo khi-taa-baa)

رَّبِّ ٱلسَّمَـٰوَٰتِ وَٱلْأَرْضِ وَمَا بَيْنَهُمَا ٱلرَّحْمَـٰنِ لَا يَمْلِكُونَ مِنْهُ خِطَابًا ﴿٣٧﴾

"The Day that the Spirit (i.e., Gibreel) and the angels will stand in rows, they will not speak except for one whom the Most Merciful permits, and he will say what is correct."

(Yow-ma ya-qoo-moor-roo-hoo wal-ma-laa-ee-ka-too saf-fun laa ya-ta-kal-lamoo-na il-laa mun a-thee-na la-hoor-rah-maa-noo wa-qaa-la sa-waa-baa)

يَوْمَ يَقُومُ ٱلرُّوحُ وَٱلْمَلَـٰٓئِكَةُ صَفًّا لَّا يَتَكَلَّمُونَ إِلَّا مَنْ أَذِنَ لَهُ ٱلرَّحْمَـٰنُ وَقَالَ صَوَابًا ﴿٣٨﴾

Sounds great, right?

The rewards of Jannah are **amazing**, but Allah reminds us in these next ayaat that they are **not free.**

On Yowmul-Qiyaamah every creation will come in front of Allah, even the **angels**, the **jinn**, and all the **animals** that were ever created.

No one will be allowed to speak without Allah's permission. If Allah gives permission to speak to anyone, they will only say what is **correct and true**.

Allah is the one who will be in **total control** on that day.

"That is the true (i.ee. certain) day; so, he who wills may take to his Lord a (way of) return."

(Thaa-lee-kal-yow-mool-haq fa-mun shaa-at-ta-kha-tha ee-laa rab-bee-hee ma-aa-baa)

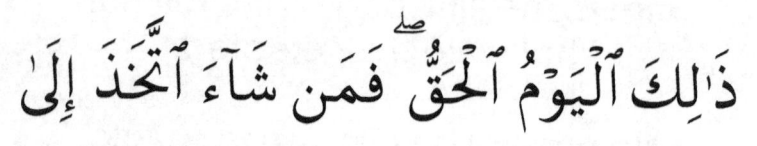

ذَٰلِكَ ٱلْيَوْمُ ٱلْحَقُّ ۖ فَمَن شَآءَ ٱتَّخَذَ إِلَىٰ رَبِّهِۦ مَـَٔابًا ﴿٣٩﴾

So, Allah tells us...

Yowmul-Qiyaamah is **real**. Anyone who wants to be **welcomed into Allah's Jannah** on that day must work hard in this life, doing what Allah told them to do, and staying away from what Allah has forbidden them to do.

"Indeed, We have warned you of a near punishment on the day when a man will observe what his hands have put forth, and the disbeliever will say, "Oh, I wish that I were dust!"

(In-naa an-thar-naa-koom 'a-thaa-ban qa-ree-baa yow-ma yan-thoo-rool-mar-oo maa qad-da-mut ya-daa-hoo wa-ya-qoo-lool-kaa-fee-roo yaa lay-ta-nee koon-too too-raa-baa)

إِنَّآ أَنذَرْنَٰكُمْ عَذَابًا قَرِيبًا يَوْمَ يَنظُرُ ٱلْمَرْءُ مَا قَدَّمَتْ يَدَاهُ وَيَقُولُ ٱلْكَافِرُ يَٰلَيْتَنِى كُنتُ تُرَٰبًۢا ۝

Otherwise be warned...

On Yowmul-Qiyaamah the disbelievers will see the **harvest of their deeds** and realize they did not prepare for this day, but then it will be too late.

Then all they will have left to say is...

"I wish that I were dust!!"

Why will they want to be dust?

They will say this because one of the first things to happen on Yowmul-Qiyaamah is that Allah will give all the weak animals a chance to get their rights, then Allah will command that **all the animals become dust** (because animals are not rewarded or punished with Jannah or Jahannam).

For example, a hornless sheep who was hurt by a sheep with horns, will be given the chance to fight back equally with the other sheep that harmed it, and then both sheep will become dust.

So, when the disbelievers see that the animals become dust, and they do not have to go to Jahannam, they will wish to be dust as well.

They think that if they are dust, they will not have to be judged by Allah, but **they will not get their wish.**

The End!

Suratun-Naba' Review

What is Suratun-Naba' about?

Suratun-Naba' tells us that disbelievers argue about Yowmul-Qiyaamah, but Allah shows them in the creation that He is capable of doing everything He intends.

In what city was Suratun-Naba' revealed?

Makkah

What is so special about Suratun-Naba'?

It is the first surah in the 30th Juz' of the Qur'an.

What does Allah ask the disbelievers in Suratun-Naba'?

What are you arguing about, the Great News?

What is the Great News?

That Yowmul-Qiyaamah is coming.

When will the disbelievers be convinced that Yowmul-Qiyaamah is real?

When it actually happens, but then it will be too late.

What are the 11 examples of Allah's power to create that are given in Suratun-Naba'?

1. Earth
2. Mountains
3. Pairs (male and female)
4. Sleep
5. Night
6. Day
7. Sky (seven heavens)
8. Sun
9. Rain
10. Grain & vegetation
11. Lush gardens

Why does Allah mention these examples?

Because they show that Allah is capable of doing whatever He intends. The complexity and magnitude of this current creation proves that such a great event is easy for Allah to do.

What does Allah tell us about Yowmul-Qiyaamah in this surah?

1. It has an appointed time that only Allah knows.
2. It will start when Angel Israfeel blows the horn.
3. The heavens will open like gates and the mountains will disappear.

What has been prepared for the disbelievers?

Jahannam

What does Allah tell us about Jahannam?

1. Those who enter it will stay forever.
2. Time is not the same.
3. There will be nothing cool there.
4. There will be two drinks.
5. Allah will give them nothing but increase in punishment.

What are the two drinks in Jahannam?

Boiling water and intensely cold, putrid liquid made from the sweat, tears, and pus from infected wounds.

Why will those who deny Yowmul-Qiyaamah be punished so severely?

They did not think they would have to answer for their deeds, and they strongly denied the message.

Is this a fair punishment?

Yes, Allah tells us this is the right punishment for these people.

Can there be terrible consequences for just having incorrect beliefs in this life?

Yes. In the story of the careless farmer, he faced starvation and homelessness just because he did not believe that he needed to put the work in to learn how to farm correctly.

How are disbelievers like the careless farmer?

They do not put in the work to get a good harvest of deeds, so they have nothing to earn Jannah or keep away Jahannam on Yowmul-Qiyaamah.

What will be in store for the believers on Yowmul-Qiyaamah?

They will enter Jannah and be given everything that their hearts desire. They will have lush gardens to live in, delicious fruits to eat, beautiful companions of the same age to live with, cups to drink from that never empty, and they will never hear anyone saying bad things or lying (like what they used to hear in this life). They will not want or need anything else, and this reward will last forever.

Is getting the rewards of Jannah easy?

No, you need to do work in this life in order to get the reward in the next life.

Who will talk on Yowmul-Qiyaamah?

No one will speak except those that Allah gives permission to, and they will only say what is true and correct.

What will the disbelievers wish on Yowmul-Qiyaamah?

They will wish to be dust.

Why will they want to be dust?

Because the animals will be turned to dust, and they will not face the punishment of Jahannam. So, the disbelievers hope to avoid punishment by wishing to be like the animals.

Notes to the text

[1] Allah has said that we should seek refuge with Him from Shaytaan before reciting Qur'aan by saying, "A-oo-thoo-bill-laa-he-min-nash-shay-taan-nir-ra-jeem".

(So when you) want to recite the Qur'an, seek refuge with Allah from Shaytaan, the outcast (the cursed one). (Qur'aan 16:98)

The majority of scholars state that reciting this phrase, known as the Isti'aathah in Arabic (pronounced Is-ti-`aa-thah), is recommended and not required, and therefore, not reciting it does not constitute a sin. However, Rasulullah ﷺ always said the Isti`aathah. In addition, the Isti`aathah wards off the evil of Shaytaan, which is necessary; the rule is that the means needed to implement a requirement of the religion is itself also required. And when one says, "I seek refuge with Allah from the cursed devil." Then this will suffice.
(Tafseer Ibn Kathir)

[2] Saying the Basmallah, "Bis-mil-laa-hir-rah-maa-nir-ra-heem" before reciting any surah, except for the ninth, Suratut-Towba, which does not have the Basmallah in the beginning, is agreed upon by all scholars, past and present.

Bibliography

1. Tafseer Ibn Kathir (Abridged), English translation by Shaykh Safiur-Rahman Al-Mubarakpuri, Darussalam Publishers, 2000

2. Sahih Al-Bukhari, English translation by Dr. Muhammed Muhsin Khan, Islamic University, Al-Medina Al-Munawwara, Kazi Publications, 1986

3. Sahih Muslim, English translation by Abdul Hamid Siddiqi, Shaykh Muhammad Ashraf Publishers, 1990

4. The Qur'aan (English translation), Saheeh International, Almunatada Alislami, Abul Qasim Publishing House, 2012

Mini Tafseer Book Series
Give the Gift of Understanding Juz 'Amma
Special Features:
* Great introduction to the Qur'aan for children
* Easy explanation of Islaam for new Muslims
* One surah per book (37 suwaar + Faatiha)
* Little known facts/trivia about each surah
* Inspiring Qur'aanic stories of the prophets
* Arabic vocabulary words from each surah
* Detailed Qur'aan & Hadith and references
* Mini grammar lessons relevent to the surah
* Coloring pages and worksheets in every book
Complete Explanation of
Juz 'Amma
38 Book Set
Visit our web site to view book previews
and learn more about our products.
www.ad-duha.org